Rory McGrath cut his teeth in Test cricket while f̲ to a particularly nasty bouncer from Joel Garner. As he has the distinction of having the first teeth to be ca̲ England. Chiefly known as a defensive batsman — w̲ criticized for his batting in the dressing-room he wo̲u̲l̲d̲ ̲g̲e̲t onto the defensive — he is nevertheless capable of a mean cover drive and a rather selfish reverse sweep. He also has an extremely useful pair of hands — in fact he rarely goes out without them.

❊ ❊ ❊ ❊ ❊ ❊ ❊ ❊ ❊ ❊ ❊ ❊ ❊ ❊ ❊

Peter Fincham prides himself on his knowledge of incredibly trivial facts about cricket. He plays for the Little Humpingham 2nd XI and can be found most Saturday nights in the saloon bar of the Cricketing Arms regaling all and sundry with the record for the fastest 50 scored on a wet Wednesday in May by a one-legged Middlesex No. 11. The rest of the team can usually be found in the public bar of the Dog and Duck. Peter's friends call him the 'walking *Wisden*', i.e. he's thick, heavy-going, yellowish in colour, and doesn't change much from year to year.

❊ ❊ ❊ ❊ ❊ ❊ ❊ ❊ ❊ ❊ ❊ ❊ ❊ ❊ ❊

Ian Moore hails from Inverness-shire and is the latest in a long line of fine Scottish cricketers which begins and ends with Mike Denness. A lethal first-change leg-spinner, Ian is notorious for his ability to keep batsmen pinned down for long periods — which certainly makes it easier to bowl them out. The highlight of Ian's career so far was in a charity match when he got the opportunity to bowl to Ian Botham and had the famous all-rounder in all kinds of trouble — assaulting policemen, drug offences, and resisting arrest.

Illustrated by Nigel Paige

Cricket

MADE SILLY

Rory McGrath, Peter Fincham and Ian Moore

CENTURY

LONDON · MELBOURNE · AUCKLAND · JOHANNESBURG

Design/Gwyn Lewis
Graphics/Ian Sandom

First published in 1986 by Century Hutchinson Ltd,
Brookmount House, 62–65 Chandos Place, Covent Garden,
London WC2N 4NW

Century Hutchinson Publishing Group (Australia) Pty Ltd,
PO Box 496, 16–22 Church Street, Hawthorn, Victoria 3122

Century Hutchinson Group (NZ) Ltd,
PO Box 40–086, Glenfield, Auckland 10, New Zealand

Century Hutchinson Group (SA) Pty Ltd,
PO Box 337, Bergvlei, 2012 South Africa

ISBN 0 7126 9580 X (paper)
ISBN 0 7126 1578 4 (cased)

Filmset by Deltatype, Ellesmere Port
Printed in Great Britain in 1986 by
Hazell, Watson & Viney Ltd, Aylesbury, Bucks

Preface

**By the Former Chairman of the Selectors,
Alec Bedser-Trucks**

WHY PLAY CRICKET?

There are those who maintain that spending hour after hour wandering aimlessly around a large expanse of grass, occasionally trying to hit a ball in the right direction but for the most part being bored rigid is a pretty ridiculous waste of time.

However, this isn't a book about golf — if it was it would be called *Golf Made Silly*. This is a book aimed at those who like to hear the firm smack of leather on willow, and also at people who are interested in cricket.

Cricket is certainly an odd game. As the commentators often remind us, the great thing about cricket is that you never know what's going to happen next. But then that's true of most of life except, of course, for the latter episodes of *'Tales of the Unexpected.'*

Cricket is, after all, our national sport. When whoever it was said that the Battle of Waterloo was won on the playing fields of Eton, presumably it was cricket he was referring to . . . or possibly football . . . or perhaps he just had a very poor sense of geography.

But I digress . . . Why play cricket?

There must be an answer, and perhaps *Cricket Made Silly* will provide it.

Then again, perhaps it won't.

As my old father used to say: 'Whatever else you do in life, son — don't quote your parents.'

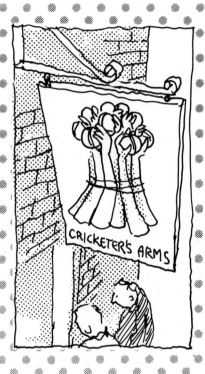

The Most Famous Cricket Joke . . .

. . . apart from the England side's scores in recent Test matches . . . concerns a village cricket team who come to play the most important match of the year and find themselves a man short. The captain is in earnest conversation about the problem when the horse which was there to pull the heavy roller (this is quite an old joke) says that it would be quite prepared to make up the numbers.

Naturally the captain is somewhat taken aback by this but, on asking the horse two or three questions, he discovers that the horse, apart from being able to talk, does know a bit about the game.

The village team goes into bat first and has a disastrous time. With hardly any runs on the board and nine wickets down, the captain decides to take a chance and puts the horse in at number 11.

The horse is magnificent. Cover drives, hooks, leg glances, straight drives, sweeps, he can do them all. Fearless against fast bowling and able to cope with any sort of spin he soon knocks up a century and looks like staying there forever until he is left without a partner who is bowled out to the great relief of the village team's opponenents.

When they come in to bat the other side rapidly race towards the village team's total. With the light fading towards evening but with the prospect of defeat staring him in the face, the captain of the village side is running out of ideas. None of his bowlers seeming able to contain the opposition.

Suddenly he thinks of the horse who did so well as a batsman. He runs over to the horse who has been fielding at long leg for most of the innings and asks him if by any chance he would care to have a bowl.

'Don't be silly', says the horse, 'Who's ever heard of a horse bowling?'

The History of Cricket

Most people can tell you that cricket was first played in about 1760 at Hambledon, Hampshire. Which just goes to show how wrong most people can be, since it wasn't.

Indeed, it is quite possible that cricket goes back as far as the Stone Age — a primitive, distant era even before Kerry Packer burst onto the scene.

Early Man (or Opening Man as he called himself), bored with bowling body-line rocks and leg-breaks at dinosaurs, looked for some recreation to occupy his spare time.

Armed with a club in his hand, muscular, powerful and looking for all the world like a slightly more refined version of Ian Botham, he inevitably came to see himself as a batsman.

From then all it required was twenty-one other men, the invention of the ball, stumps, pitch, heavy roller and some sponsorship for the game of cricket to get going.

Is this how it happened? We will never know.

All that has survived are the wretched cave paintings made by the boy who was supposed to be keeping the score. Were great catches made at nasty, brutish and short-leg? Did early man wear a helmet to protect himself from sabre-toothed West Indians? Was there a prolonged stoppage during the Ice Age?

Who can say? The true origins of cricket are lost in the mists of time (when the umpires first had to use their light meters).

But whatever else can be said about cricket, it is a truly English game. Indeed, like nearly all sports (e.g. football) cricket was invented by the English, and unlike football we're still better at it than the Italians, West Germans and a number of South American countries which lie outside the *Test Match Special* broadcasting range.

The idea of cricket was to make it so English, so quintessentially Anglo-Saxon, so . . . dull, that no other country would be interested in playing it.

And it nearly worked!

Unfortunately there was something called the British Empire. And towards the end of the 19th century, when the colonists and the natives finally stopped fighting each other, the natives were taught to play cricket.

And the rest, as they say . . . is what snooker players use when they can't reach the ball.

Fit for Cricket

Despite the impression you may have got watching it on television, cricket is in fact a sport. Yes, a sport. Played therefore by sportsmen. Yes, sportsmen. 'But aren't sportsmen usually fit and athletic?' I hear you say. 'Well', *I* say, 'Can you stop asking questions when I'm trying to write something.' Yes, cricketers are athletes. 'But', you say to me, 'why do all cricketers on telly look like pot-bellied slobs? Is this a distortion of the TV cameras? Is it protective padding that they wear around their middle and their jowls?' No. They are in fact pot-bellied slobs, and you're interrupting me again. The fact is that cricketers are fit in their own way. They're not fit like footballers, runners, swimmers, or bus conductors . . . but they do have to be able to run at least 22 yards, sometimes more than once a day.

HOME TRAINER

Here is a table of energy use for different sports and cricket.

Activity	KCals used in 10 minutes continuous action for 11 stone man
Walking upstairs	175
Cross-country skiing	135
Skipping	125
Running (7.5 m.p.h.)	125
Screwing (man on top)	120
Screwing (woman on top)	15
Screwing (man and woman on top)	300
Opening vacuum-wrapped bacon	80
Trying to get served in a pub on the Friday lunchtime before Christmas	140
Getting up and switching channels again and again, trying to find something decent to watch on TV on a Saturday night	90
Talking about getting round to taking up some form of exercise in the New Year	70
Avoiding that smarmy, and prematurely balding solicitor at a drinks party	100
Being in a coma	50
Listening to Radio 3	40
Being dead	30
Appearing on Radio 3	20
Test cricket	0

The Laws of Cricket

Cricket is unique among sports in not having rules but laws, a fact which is supposed to signify something or other. The Laws of Cricket can be found on approximately page 967 of *Wisden*, and it has to be said that if you've got that far you're a glutton for punishment.

Cricket has traditionally been played in the 'spirit' of the game, i.e. the players never cheat and never try to take unfair advantage of their opponents. It is for this reason that it is so dull to play and completely doomed as a spectator sport.

Law 1
The Players

The object of cricket is very simple and so are many of the people who play it.

A match is played between two sides of eleven players, one of whom shall be the captain.

In the event of eleven players not being available at any time, the captain shall first 'give them another five minutes', then make a series of frantic phone calls, then ask the opposing captain if he wouldn't mind lending him a couple of fielders.

The object of the game is basically to get out of doing the shopping or cutting the lawn on a Saturday afternoon.

Law 2 The Umpires

The game is presided over by two umpires. They usually look like overweight lab assistants with ladies' sun hats on. The umpires make their decisions known by a series of gestures as follows.

'Me and the boys will now do "In the Mood". A one-two-three-four.'

'Please may I be excused?'

'Who's stolen my parrot?'

'Taxi!'

'Excuse me, I've farted . . .'

'OK Which hand is it in?'

'Oooh, look — a finger!'

'If I ruled the world, every day would be the first day of Spring.'

'Ugh! Bloody dogs.'

Law 3
The Scorer

The scorer is usually a quiet, withdrawn character with National Health glasses who obviously hasn't got anything better to do at weekends than work out people's bowling averages and whose ultimate ambition is to meet Bill Frindle. His catchphrase is 'Bowler's name?' In fact he rarely says anything else.

Law 4
Intervals

There shall be an interval for lunch and an interval for tea and there are all sorts of complicated rules about not taking tea if there's only two wickets to fall and more than twenty-five overs still need to be bowled before six o'clock.

These can be completely ignored: tea is taken when the lady who's been making sandwiches since 1947 says it will be taken, and God help any visiting team which tries to interfere with the arrangements.

Law 5
Declarations

The captain of the batting side may declare the innings closed at any time. While sitting in the pavilion waiting to bat, he can also declare the innings an almost complete waste of time and wonder why on earth he goes on week after week with the same shower of incompetents who haven't won a game since men were first sent into space — which might be a very good fate for them, in fact.

Law 6
No-Ball

The no-ball law is a complicated one and umpires are advised not to try to come to terms with it for fear of getting confused. In practice, a no-ball is only called on that one ball in six when the umpire remembers that he is supposed to watch where the bowler's feet land in relation to the popping crease.

Law 7
Timed Out

This is arguably the most obscure way of getting out and is only included so that know-alls can show off the fact that they can remember all ten ways of being out at cricket.

Ways of Getting Out

(1) Run Out

When you lose your wicket by means of the bails being removed before you have successfully made your ground, you have been run out. It takes two people to do this:

(1) The member of the opposite team who throws down your stumps.

(2) The other batsman.

It is an inviolable rule of being run out that it is always the other chap's fault, unless of course it is the other chap who gets run out — in which case it is his fault as well.

There are two principal ways to avoid being run out:

(a) Concentrate on running between the wickets.

(b) Concentrate on *not* running between the wickets.

The latter approach is known as 'standing your ground' or 'Boycott's technique'.

When you call for a run to your partner it is vital that what you say is clear, decisive and unambiguous. Similarly his replies. A typical exchange might be as follows:

'Stop!'

'Wait!'

'Come!'

'Yes!'

'No!'

'Pardon!'

'Your shout!'

'You shit!'

'Sorry!'

This to be followed by the long, sad walk back to the pavilion.

(2) L.B.W.

Just as the person responsible for running you out is normally the other batsman, i.e. a member of your own team, so the person who gets you out l.b.w. is normally the blinkered idiot in white who stands at the other end of the pitch — the umpire. Generally speaking, he is also a member of your own team.

Of all the laws of cricket the law governing l.b.w. is one of the most complicated and difficult to grasp. Fortunately, for lesser grades of cricket in which the umpires are drawn from members of the batting side who go in further down the order, it is replaced by an easier version — 'If the ball strikes the batsman on the pad roughly in line with the wicket and the fielding side all appeal in unison, imagine what it would be like to face him in the pavilion during tea and for God's sake give him not out.'

(3) Bowled

Being bowled is probably the most annoying way of getting out because it's really very difficult to pin the blame on anyone except yourself.

There's something peculiarly sickening about the decisive click with which the ball removes the bails when you seem to have played a perfectly respectable forward defensive shot, apart of course from the nine-inch gap you inadvertently left between bat and pad.

Unfortunately the bails fall off the stumps quite easily, so a little bit of Blue Tack is recommended if you want to stay in longer.

(4) Caught

As well as possessing the remarkable quality of swinging through the air for no apparent reason, another extraordinary thing a cricket ball can do is hit the upper edge of the bat yet somehow contrive to give the batsman a nasty bruise on the forearm. Furthermore, this bruise has a strange way of clearing up as soon as the umpire gives the batsman not out.

In the old days conscientious batsmen would 'walk' before the umpire's decision. With some of the fast bowling you get these days it might be better to walk before the bowler finishes his run-up.

Remember what our parents told us, 'Don't try to run before you can walk.' From the point of view of cricket, this advice can be completely ignored.

(5) Hit wicket

This is an absolutely maddening way to get out. What happens is that the batsman, while attempting a shot, inadvertently hits the stumps with his bat, thus removing the bails. He is therefore judged out. What generally follows is that the batsman, in a moment of extreme anger, takes a swing at the stumps and knocks them over. This doesn't make the slightest difference – there's no such offence as 'Hit wicket twice'.

(6) Hit the ball twice

There is, however, an offence called 'Hit the ball twice'. The only occasion on which you are likely to do this is when the ball looks like hitting your stumps after you first make contact with it.

Oddly enough, this is the only occasion on which you are actually allowed to hit the ball twice – which rather makes nonsense of this rule.

(7) Obstructing the field

Another obscure and exotic way of getting out. And a remarkable achievement too – a cricket field is usually more than a hundred yards across, so you'd need to be the size of Colin Milburn to obstruct it.

(8) Stumped

The batsman who is stumped, like the batsman who is l.b.w., nearly always believes himself to be unfairly dismissed. This is because in the split second it takes the wicket-keeper to remove the bails, the batsman invariably thinks he has got his foot back behind the popping crease – which quite often he hasn't.

A competent batsman should always be able to avoid being stumped – by not letting his back foot drag, keeping the wicket-keeper unsighted, or even hitting the ball.

(9) Handled the ball

A pretty blatant offence which leaves little scope for the batsman to complain about unfair dismissal. Batsmen frequently 'handle the ball' when they pick it up and chuck it back to the bowler after playing a forward defensive shot. They get away with this because the ball is dead – or possibly because the umpire is dead and hasn't noticed what went on.

(10) Timed out

Finally, the most obscure of all ways of getting out. If you are the next man in and a wicket falls and you take more than two minutes to get from the pavilion to the crease, you are liable to be 'timed out'. If you are batting and your partner calls for a run and you take more than two minutes to get from one end of the pitch to the other, you are more likely to be 'run out'.

These are the only two ways in which it is possible to get out without ever facing a ball – and thus, from certain points of view, the ideal ways of forfeiting your wicket.

· Landmarks in Cricketing History ·

The invention of one-day cricket . . .

One-day cricket has always existed, but in the past the phrase usually referred to matches between a county side featuring either Oxford or Cambridge University, which were lucky if they lasted beyond teatime on the first day.

Then somebody had the wacky idea of inventing a competition in which the counties played each other over a maximum of 65 overs each, starting at 10.30 in the morning and ending the same evening.

This proved immensely entertaining and highly profitable, and gave cricket the vital shot in the arm it needed from every point of view.

Hence the almost total opposition to it from *Daily Telegraph* readers, retired brigadiers and bores.

Cricket Made Silly Fielding Positions

The team that isn't batting stand around in various random positions on the field. They are called fielders and it's their job to stay awake.

- Long Line of Cocaine
- Long Leg
- Long John
- Long John Silver
- Wooden Leg
- Long Off
- Jerk Off
- Bowler
- Fedora
- Panama
- Trilby
- Silly Isles
- Streaker from Crowd
- Cover
- Eiderdown
- Silly Point
- North Wicket
- Mid Wicket
- South Wicket
- Silly Mid Off
- Irrelevant Argument
- Point
- Gesticulate
- Waggle Tongue
- Silly Mid On
- Cow Pat
- Batsman
- Umpire
- Umpire
- Stick It Up Yer Jumpire
- 1st Slip
- 2nd Slip
- Banana Skin
- Arse Over Tit
- Third Man
- Orson Welles
- Deep Fine Leg
- Left Leg In
- Left Leg Out
- In, out, in, out, Shake it all about

Cricket Made Silly Quiz

A quiz for all cricket buffs and for those who play with their clothes on.

(1) **Does the word 'cricket' derive from . . . ?**

(a) the French word 'criquet' which literally means 'the English game of cricket'

(b) the old English word 'cricc' a low stool (i.e. what is produced when you face fast bowling)

(c) the word 'cricket', meaning a type of grasshopper that runs off at the first sign of rain

(2) **Why is there no such position as 'silly long leg'?**

(3) **Is a Chinaman . . . ?**

(a) The proprietor of a takeaway restaurant

(b) A figure, in human shape, made of porcelain

(c) An off-break bowled by a left-handed restauranteur at a right-handed ornament

(4) Three players called Mike Smith have played first-class cricket in England. Name them.

(5) When facing fast bowling, what do you think is the batsman's most important piece of equipment . . . ?

    (a) A helmet
    (b) A box
    (c) A thighpad
    (d) A bat

(6) In the 256 Test Matches between England and Australia, which country has won the least matches . . . ?

    (a) Australia
    (b) England
    (c) New Zealand

(7) Which of the following are ways of being out at cricket . . . ?

    (a) Bowled
    (b) Hit wicket
    (c) Ate umpire
    (d) Handled ball
    (e) Took more than 2 minutes to come out of the pavilion
    (f) Took more than 2 minutes to run a quick single
    (g) Took more than 2 seconds to see a fast delivery

(8) If a ball shatters on impact with the bat, how many pieces of it have to be safely held in the hands of the fielders for the batsman to be caught out?

(9) Name the Sponsors of the following competitions.

    (a)   The Nat West Trophy
    (b)   The Schweppes County Championship
    (c)   The John Player League

(10) Explain the difference between the following terms . . .

    (a)   Going round the wicket
    (b)   Going over the wicket
    (c)   Tripping over the wicket

(11) If it is just a silly stereotype to see all Yorkshiremen as dour, stubborn, selfish, self-interested and humourless, how do you explain Geoffrey Boycott?

(12) If it takes 3 days to complete a County Match, 5 days for a Test Match, why is a week a long time in politics?

Batting for Beginners

Cricketing manuals are full of painstaking descriptions of the perfect forward defensive shot and the correct way to pull (see also *Sex Made Silly*). These can be almost completely disregarded. The truly bad batsman has a strictly limited number of shots at his disposal, which is just as well, since he faces a strictly limited number of balls before getting out.

The Prod

(a) The shot you should use for about the first ten minutes of your innings and thereafter whenever a new bowler is brought on.

(b) A non-Catholic in Belfast.

The Drive

(a) The shot you rehearse immaculately while the wicket-keeper is returning the ball to the bowler, having just made a complete fool of yourself attempting a cover drive for four.

(b) A group of geriatrics playing cards together.

The Slash

(a) An attempted cut, or perhaps a late cut. Often a cut so late that it could be construed as a pull at the next delivery.

(b) What you do behind the sightscreen between overs.

The Slog

(a) The hell-for-leather heave at the ball you allow yourself every couple of overs, often referred to as an 'agricultural' shot on the basis that if you actually made contact with the ball it would end up hitting the farmer in the next field.

(b) Writing *Made Silly* books.

The Hook

(a) The panicky attempt to stop the ball hitting you in the face which — if successful — looks like a brave and controlled shot to the boundary.

(b) A place in Holland.

The Push

(a) The slightly timid, half-defensive, half-attacking, neither-one-thing-nor-the-other SDP sort of shot with which you try to get a quick single and let your partner face the bowling.

(b) What David Gower should have got after the 1986 Caribbean tour.

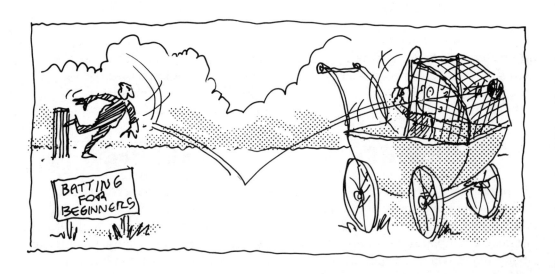

Cricketing Stances

FORWARD DEFENSIVE

Feet well forward on coffee table, eyes directly in line with screen — the classic stance for a Sunday afternoon when you were supposed to be sweeping out the garden shed.

ON-THE-DEFENSIVE

Pathetic attempt to defend above to indignant wife.

SWEEP

Half-hearted attempt to tidy garden shed while listening to Test match on the radio.

REVERSE SWEEP

Absent-minded untidying of garden shed again while in trance induced by radio commentary.

Cricketing

There are various items of cricketing equipment — bat, pads, gloves, box, interesting book to read while waiting to bat — which it is essential that you have. Failing that, it is essential that somebody else has them so that you can borrow them.

Cricketers are by and large great borrowers, helping themselves to each other's equipment and anecdotes in equal amounts.

In recent years it has seemed that batsmen will have to wear ever-increasing amounts of equipment. When Mike Brearley first appeared in a helmet in 1976, he was greeted with hoots of derision. Mind you, he was having dinner in the Dorchester at the time. Nowadays helmets are as essential to batsmen as they are to policemen, and it may not be long before the bat is replaced by a cricketing version of the riot shield.

With fast bowling getting more and more aggressive, even club cricketers are recommended to have some sort of protection these days. I suggest the Universal All-Risks policy from Unit Life Assurance, of which by coincidence my brother is an agent.

Equipment

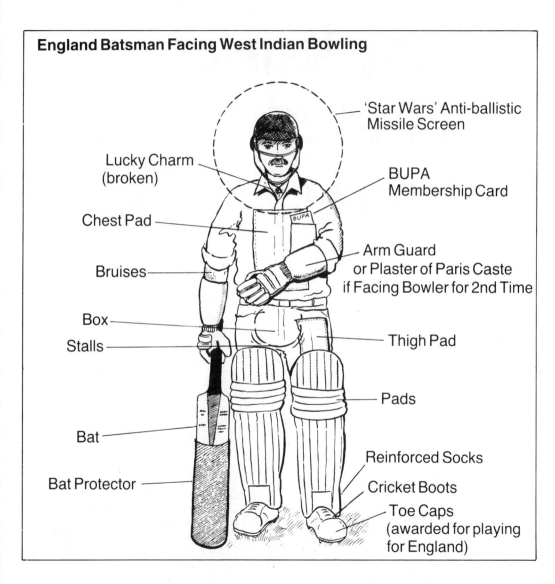

England Batsman Facing West Indian Bowling

'Star Wars' Anti-ballistic Missile Screen

Lucky Charm (broken)

BUPA Membership Card

Chest Pad

Bruises

Arm Guard or Plaster of Paris Caste if Facing Bowler for 2nd Time

Box

Stalls

Thigh Pad

Pads

Bat

Reinforced Socks

Cricket Boots

Bat Protector

Toe Caps (awarded for playing for England)

The Decline of English Fast Bowling

The vexed question of why the English can't produce decent fast bowlers is one of our great national mysteries like 'How can we stop our industrial decline?' 'Why hasn't Selina Scott got a boyfriend?' and 'Which sport does Peter West actually know something about?' Hour after hour is spent discussing the problem in pubs, factories and offices — which is in fact one of the chief reasons for the industrial decline . . . prompting the thought that if only we could produce a couple of Malcolm Marshalls and a Joel Garner, perhaps we could make hi-fi equipment more cheaply than the Japanese . . .

But I digress. The decline of English fast bowling is a sad and sorry tale.

Trevor Bailey is of the opinion that the last truly great English fast bowler was Harold Larwood.

Fred Trueman is of the opinion that the last truly great English fast bowler was Fred Trueman.

Fred Trueman looks back to the days when he bore down on the opposition at full stretch.

And the other commentators resign themselves to the fact that now he simply bores them.

What can be done? There are those who believe that the English physique is simply inadequate for fast bowling and that we should concentrate on developing the talents of those who are British citizens but hail from remote, less refined parts of the Commonwealth.

But others feel that the Welsh simply aren't up to it.

Cricketing Counties

There are two sorts of counties: Major Counties and Minor Counties.

In cricketing terms, the Major Counties seem to have bestowed on themselves the honour of taking part in the County Championship in a fairly arbitrary fashion, without taking much account of size or population.

Quite why Devon should be saddled with the title Minor County while its rather smaller neighbour Somerset can call upon the services of Ian Botham and Viv Richards remains a mystery.

Anyway, there it is. There are seventeen Major Counties, and a perfectly harmless half-hour can be spent on any long car journey trying to remember the names of them all (during which it's quite likely that you'll pass through at least three or four).

Most people can think of about sixteen and then get stuck. Derbyshire is usually the one people forget, being arguably the dullest of the lot . . .

Middlesex

The only county to have won the championship several times after ceasing to exist.

Yorkshire

Maintains a policy of only fielding players born within the county boundary – which can be found at Headingley. Never wins anything.

Lancashire

A good one-day team, as in the expression, 'One day this lot might win something'.

Kent

Known as the 'garden of England', as a result of which there is a tree growing in the middle of the county ground.

Gloucestershire

The cheese 'Double Gloucester' isn't named after the year when they won both the championship and the Nat West Trophy . . . since they never have.

Leicestershire

Another county with cheesy connotations. Red Leicester is in fact named after the expression on the locals' faces when they see how badly they fare in the championship year after year.

Sussex

Actually two counties, West Sussex and East Sussex. You might deduce from this that they'd be twice as good as other counties. You'd be wrong.

Northamptonshire

Easily confused with Nottinghamshire.

Nottinghamshire

Easily confused with Northamptonshire.

Derbyshire

A very dull county indeed.

Somerset

Home of Ian Botham, who brought a new meaning to the phrase 'concentrating on your line'.

THE SCOREBOARD

The simplest form of scoreboard is a device with a few rows of digits that the scorer's son is supposed to look after all afternoon. Nobody believes the score on such a scoreboard as the son usually gets bored after about an hour and leaves it showing 55 for 3 when the batting team are trying to remember if they are 189 or 199 with one wicket left.

More complicated scoreboards are to be found on Test and County grounds. They tell you useful things like the total, the number of wickets down etc but you generally can't see these figures very easily because they are all mixed up with useless information that only scorers themselves are interested in, like the score of the last batsman in, what the score was when the last wicket fell, and so on.

If you are lucky the scoreboard will tell you what you actually want to know, i.e. how many runs are needed to win.

However, because cricket competitions are so complicated and the average spectator is used to television coverage, these days scoreboards are having to get even more elaborate.

The Modern Scoreboard

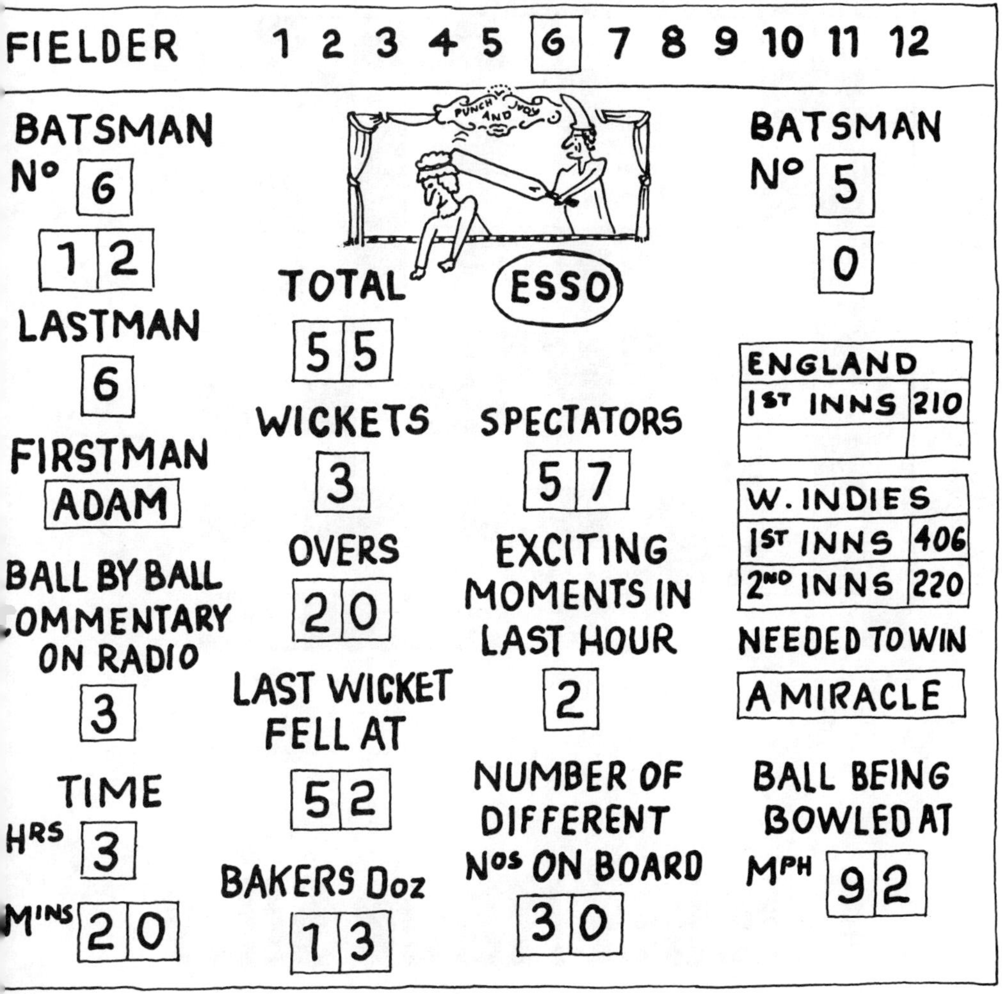

FIELDER   1 2 3 4 5 **6** 7 8 9 10 11 12

BATSMAN No **6**

1 **2**

LASTMAN **6**

FIRSTMAN **ADAM**

BALL BY BALL COMMENTARY ON RADIO **3**

TIME
HRS **3**
MINS **2** **0**

TOTAL **5** **5**

WICKETS **3**

OVERS **2** **0**

LAST WICKET FELL AT **5** **2**

BAKERS Doz **1** **3**

ESSO

SPECTATORS **5** **7**

EXCITING MOMENTS IN LAST HOUR **2**

NUMBER OF DIFFERENT Nos ON BOARD **3** **0**

BATSMAN No **5**

0

ENGLAND	
1ST INNS	210

W. INDIES	
1ST INNS	406
2ND INNS	220

NEEDED TO WIN **A MIRACLE**

BALL BEING BOWLED AT
MPH **9** **2**

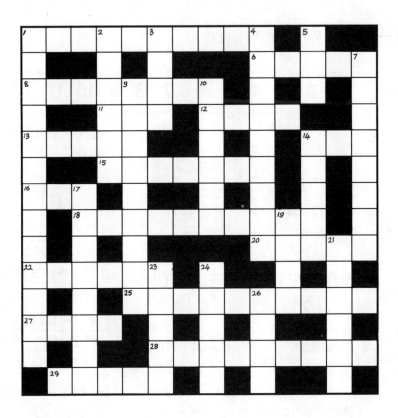

Cricket Made Silly

Across

1/ Senior cricket club confuses ebony realm. (10)

6/ A bowler to worry batsmen, a captain to worry farmers. (5)

8/ Teacher's pet sits close, but not quite close enough. (4, 4)

11/ A violin in the pocket of your cricket togs? (3)

12/ A load of balls. (5)

13/ Arise and possibly go to S. Africa. (5)

14/ One side of cricket seen in allegory. (3)

15/ Go back and stand another drink. (7)

16/ Cancelled for nothing and two farthings. (3)

18/ Such is the competition for the Sheffield Shield, it could be the World Cup. (10)

20/ Calm periods when students are mixed up with us. (5)

22/ Soldiers' fast spell shows ability. (6)

25/ Something to pick up on a cricket field or a Club 18–30 holiday. (4, 6)

27/ Found in eleven and seven, though both are odd. (4)

28/ Collections of groups of cricketers break for coffee. (9)

29/ Remains when stumps are drawn, quartered and burnt at the stake? (5)

Down

1/ Yorkshire, Kent and Nottinghamshire, say. (5, 8)

2/ An oddball from city queen. (6)

3/ Oriental cross before it goes out. (4)

4/ Necessary German food with curly tail. (9)

5/ Best you can make from one strike is point-nine. (3)

7/ Goes about zero gravity lithium balls. (8)

9/ Oddly lions meet at signpost. (8)

10/ Caribbean coffee does this. (6)

14/ Even students are separated by first mate. (5)

17/ Cricketers made by endless fig-trees. (8)

19/ Bird said to make this performance. (4)

21/ Aussie cricketer has girl running to shelter. (6)

23/ Two-pointed hat subdues. (5)

24/ One-time Australian captain names golf competition. (5)

26/ thought from a sordid easterner. (4)

* Solution on p. 96

Crossword

The MCC

As you might expect, the MCC (Marylebone Cricket Club) has its headquarters at Lord's, which is in St John's Wood.

The MCC is a name under which English teams used to play when abroad, until someone quite rightly woke up to the fact that this was like expecting the England football team to tour under the name Willesden Football Club, because they play their home matches in nearby Wembley.

This would clearly be an absurd idea, though Willesden have in fact achieved some good results lately — which is more than can be said for England.

Nevertheless the MCC is undoubtedly a distinguished and august body — well, as a matter of fact it functions throughout the rest of the year as well.

Membership of the MCC is strictly limited. Only those who apply are allowed to join.

The broad yellow and orange stripes of the club tie almost personify all that is great, traditional, red-blooded and manly about British Cricket. Incidentally it is exactly the same tie as Wardlebury Junior Girl's School.

Famous Cricket Grounds
in England

One of the pleasures of watching a Test Match series on television is that each match comes from a different ground, and on television Trent Bridge looks as different from Headingley as, say, No. 2 Court at Wimbledon looks from No. 3 Court.

LORD'S

Lord's is the headquarters of cricket and is best known for its Tavern and ridge, both of which have been removed. From the point of view of the television viewer, distinctive features include a remarkably good view of the pitch from the top of the pavilion, and a series of advertising hoardings around the boundary proclaiming the virtues of assorted insurance and cigarette companies.

THE OVAL

Called the Oval because of its elliptical shape (which doesn't actually come across on TV), this historic ground is situated in a picturesque part of South London between a series of main roads and a gas works.

OLD TRAFFORD

A magnificent cricket ground spoiled only by being in Manchester, where it always rains, and by the fact that Manchester United play football on it from August to May. By the way, the ground is ringed by a remarkable series of advertising hoardings.

TRENT BRIDGE

Slightly less famous ground in Nottingham, or possibly Northampton, which is easily confused with Edgbaston and Headingley if you didn't happen to look in the paper to see where the Test Match was being played this time. The television viewer gets an excellent view from directly behind the bowler's arm.

HEADINGLEY Fairly famous ground where Ian Botham won the Ashes single-handed in 1981 by allowing Bob Willis to bowl the Australians out for just over 100. Being in Yorkshire, the advertising hoardings are confined to firms situated within the county boundary.

EDGBASTON Unusual in that the TV cameras are situated at square leg and advertising has been banned by the local council . . . No, seriously, Edgbaston is exactly like all the other cricket grounds of England, except for having the unfortunate privilege of being situated in Birmingham.

· Landmarks in Cricketing History ·

Bodyline
The aim of bodyline was to strike directly at the players' bodies and appeal to what is known as the 'fear factor'. It emerged in the late 1930s, briefly outraged world opinion and got everyone talking about cricket for a few months, then faded away again.

· Landmarks in Cricketing History ·

Kerry Packer
The aim of Kerry Packer was to strike directly at the players' wallets and appeal to what is known as the 'greed factor'. He wanted to buy up the players body-and-soul, hence the so-called body-and-soul-line series. This emerged in the late 1970s, briefly outraged world opinion and got everyone talking about cricket for a few months, then faded away again.

· Scoring a Century·

For a cricketer, there's nothing quite like reaching a hundred, and indeed it's a landmark in most people's lives — you do, after all, get a telegram from the Queen.

But even if the century is merely an innings in a game of cricket, it's something to savour, reflect on, feel good about — which is why so many batsmen are out in the early hundreds while they're busy savouring, reflecting and feeling good. There are right and wrong ways to acknowledge the crowd's applause.

Acknowledging the crowd's applause

Wrong

Right

Completely wrong

Cricket Around the World

As has been explained, the original idea of cricket was not to teach it to anyone else, on the basis that, like the long line of English successes in the Oxford v Cambridge boat race, we would remain the best in the world.

Just to prove this, we took the (not very great) risk of showing the Welsh how to play. Glamorgan have been coming 17th in the Country Championship ever since.

Below is a list of countries in which cricket is either the national sport, has a keen amateur following, or is more or less completely unheard of.

Wales

Home of Glamorgan, unemployment, Tony Lewis, the hills and the valleys, the flat bits, Greg Thomas and his brother Dylan. No cricket worth speaking of played here.

France

French cricket is a bastardized form of the real game played on a litter-strewn beach between a bored father and his argumentative children in which the idea is to strike the body of the batsman rather than the wicket (see *Landmarks in Cricketing History*: Bodyline).

It is not played in France. The French answer to cricket is 'boule'. They're not very polite about our other games either.

Bulgaria

Another country in which no cricket is played.

Lower Silesia

Yet another.

West Indies

At last somewhere where cricket is played, but oddly enough, not a country. There are a number of different countries in and around the Caribbean Ocean which get together simply in order to produce the best team possible, like the Barbarians at Rugby. In fact they're rather like barbarians at cricket.

West Indian teams win in England because they cheat by getting their players to play in county sides to get used to the conditions. They win in the West Indies by playing better.

America American cricket is similar to baseball. It is played on a baseball 'diamond' between two teams called 'baseball teams'. After the ball is hit, the batsmen run round bases, baseball fashion . . . Well, let's face it, it *is* baseball.

Russia Russian cricket is run by the MCCCP instead of the MCC, so that apart from the usual reasons for dismissal, you can be caught out thinking anti-Soviet thoughts during the bowler's run up.

India A very large country usually ruled by somebody called Ghandi and directed by Richard Attenborough. India has some very good spin bowlers who do not give touring sides many runs, unlike the local cuisine which gives everyone the runs.

Sri Lanka The name of the place where Ceylon tea comes form. Sri Lankan cricket has come on by leaps and bounds in recent years, but once the bowlers have got their run-up right they should be a force to be reckoned with.

Italy Italian cricket is very simple. The fielding side bowls very aggressively and the batting side immediately goes into retreat and surrenders.

China Home of the Chinaman. Home of umpteen million Chinamen, in fact.

Australia   Australian cricket has reached such a low ebb in recent years that the selectors even took the controversial step of including a South African, Kesper Wessels, in the side. This offended a lot of people who felt that it was entirely wrong that a South African should play for Australia. He should play instead for England, like Tony Grieg and Alan Lamb.

South Africa   No longer wins any matches because (1) most of the population are not considered good enough at cricket (too black); (2) all the best players play for England and Australia; (3) none of the other countries will play against them.

Zimbabwe   Has yet to make its mark in international cricket. Might feature Phil Edmonds if he didn't play for England, and Bruce Grobbelar — if he didn't drop the ball so much.

Austria   Easily confused with Australia if you add the letters 'al' to its name, Austria is more notable for skiing than cricket. Also renowned for the Salzburg Festival, similar in many respects to the Scarborough Festival but also completely lacking in cricket. In terms of sheer dullness, Austria is the European equivalent of a county such as Derbyshire. (See *Cricketing Counties*.)

Wicket-Keeping

It is often said in praise of great cricketers, 'he made it look easy'.

This isn't the object of wicket-keeping at all. The object of wicket-keeping is to make it look difficult, like goal-keeping at football. If you make it look easy, everybody will assume that there's nothing much to it. Much better, when faced with a lowish catch a yard to your left, to take two steps to your right and then dive in an extravagant manner, scooping the ball up at the last moment when everyone thought it was going for four.

The fact of the matter is, wicket-keeping is a thankless task, second only to scoring, and if you turn up to play a game with an unfamiliar team, you should be on your guard against the captain casually asking, 'You don't happen to keep wicket, do you? Oh good.'

The true test of a wicket-keeper is his ability to stand up. This is the true test of most sportsmen in one way or other.

Wicket-keeping

Wrong

Right

HIGHEST INNINGS EVER
On top of a factory chimney in La Paz, Bolivia.

SECOND HIGHEST INNINGS EVER
One of Ian Botham's.

LOWEST INNINGS EVER
In the Mariana trench at the bottom of the Pacific Ocean. This was also the longest innings ever, as considerable delays were caused by the bails continually floating to the surface.

MOST WICKETS
Tungsten, the superweevil, ate more wickets, bails and stumps than Dennis Lillee's had hot dinners.

MOST BALLS
David Vine, during an Athletics meeting from Crystal Palace.

WOMEN'S CRICKET
No . . . I'm only pulling your leg.

GREATEST STAND
General Custer against the Sioux Indians at Little Big Horn. He made 641 runs for the third wicket before being caught in the back by an arrow.

FASTEST BALL
The British Rail Executives and Wives Ball, which took place on an Inter-City 125 between London and Bristol.

SILLIEST NAMES IN CRICKET
A disputed decision between Ashley Mallett and Wally Grout.

ONLY CRICKETER TO SCORE A HAT-TRICK IN A WORLD CUP FINAL
Geoff Hurst (West Ham and England), who, as well as being a great footballer, also opened the batting on Sunday afternoons for the Leytonstone Town 2nd XI.

OTHER CRICKETING RECORDS
'Cricket Lovely Cricket'
'Don't step on my blue suede groin protector'
'Don't go breaking my jaw'
'I left my stump in San Francisco'
'Son of Hickory Hollers Flannels'
'Trent Bridge Over Troubled Water'
'Clever Trevor Bailey'
'Ashes to Ashes'
'It Might As Well Rain Until Lunchtime On The Final Day'
etc.

Some Famous Cricketers

MIKE BREARLEY Intellectual and thinker, Mike Brearley's success as captain of Middlesex and England is often put down to his deep knowledge of psychology and his philosophical outlook. Well, it wasn't his batting, was it?

IAN BOTHAM

(We've been advised against writing anything about Ian Botham, since at the time of writing he has several libel actions pending against newspapers for suggesting he took drugs on an overseas tour. If successful, the money will come in useful for paying his fine for possession of cannabis.)

ALAN BORDER The great batsman and tactician. Handicapped at international level by having to play with the rest of the Australian team.

GEOFFREY BOYCOTT Once described by somebody as 'the greatest living Yorkshireman', 'the best batsman of all time' and 'me', Geoffrey Boycott has the ability, when on form, to bring a smile to the face of all his fellow Yorkshiremen. A rare ability, I think you'll agree.

More Famous Cricketers

PHIL EDMONDS   Has a reputation for being difficult, which basically means that he doesn't touch his forelock every time he sees the Chairman of the Selectors. This is hardly surprising, since his forelock disappeared years ago along with the rest of his hair.

DAVID GOWER   Elegantly stylish batsman with a deceptively casual approach to the game, i.e. it's even more casual than it appears. Loves wind-surfing, bobsleighing and eating in expensive restaurants. Almost everything except cricket, in fact. Tends to be defensive with journalists, but takes his aggression out on opposing bowlers. Or is it the other way round?

GRAHAM GOOCH   Phenomenally successful batsman who manages to unsettle bowlers with his extraordinary moustache.

MIKE GATTING   One of the few batsmen who still believe that the best way to deal with a bouncer is to glance it through the gully with your nose, Mike Gatting is a stocky, down-to-earth sort of fellow, who looks as if he drinks Real Ale and goes on hiking holidays in Youth Hostels. Notoriously difficult to dislodge once he manages to get his eye in — and there aren't many batsmen of his standard who wear glass eyes, in any case.

WALLY GROUT A cricketer with a remarkably silly name.

W. G. GRACE Known as the greatest batsman of them all.

DON BRADMAN Also known as the greatest batsman of them all.

JACK HOBBS Him as well.

COLIN COWDREY Known (more accurately) as *one* of the greatest batsmen of them all. Father of Chris.

CHRIS COWDREY Son of Colin.

SON OF MY FATHER A hit for Chicory Tip in 1971.

DAVID STEELE The only batsman to make his test playing debut in his late thirties and go on to become leader of the Liberal Party.

Women's Cricket

For many years women's only involvement with cricket was to make the sandwiches for the tea interval. But now there are women actually playing cricket, women's cricket clubs and even women's international cricket matches.

Mind you they still make the sandwiches as unaccountably there are no men who want to be tea-makers.

Women also claim to have invented overarm bowling, underarm deodorant and bursting into tears when given out l.b.w. All of which were later taken up very enthusiastically by men. The most famous woman cricketer of all time is Rachel Heyhoe Flint, not that anyone has ever seen her play but she does have a very silly name and appeared on *Any Questions* once or twice a few years ago.

Quite why women should want to play cricket is a mystery, especially to wives of male cricketers whose lives are made miserable enough by having to waste perfectly good Sunday afternoons watching their husbands make fools of themselves without playing the game themselves.

In fact the main enjoyment the average woman gets from cricket comes from asking her husband, 'Why didn't you hit with your bat, dear?' when he has been clean bowled for a duck by the first ball of his innings.

The Birth of a legend

A cricketing short story . . .

St. Poking-in-the-Undercarriage was one of England's oldest and best-loved public schools. It hadn't always been a public school, but a generous bequest from an old teacher had enabled it to become a public school from what it had been before . . . a public lavatory.

It was the beginning of Summer term. There birds were singing and the flowers were coming out: 'Hello, pansy! . . . Hello, ducky!' It was the term of exams, prizegivings and, of course, cricket. St. Poking had a strong cricketing tradition, and many of its old boys had walked out wearing an England sweater, only to be called back to the sports shop by the store detective.

In the first week of term it was tradition to play a trial match to decide on the 1st XI and more importantly to decide on the Captain. Not only was it a great honour to be the Captain of St. Poking's cricket team, but it also meant an almost automatic entrance into one of those old and venerable universities that were still willing to let a few people in through the back door, provided they were good at sports and regardless of the fact that they were thick as pigshit.

Two arch-rivals were the most likely candidates for the captaincy: Basil Ableloins-Skulduggery and Nigel Poxdribble. Basil was born with a silver spoon in his mouth . . . which rather terrified the midwife. He came from a very rich family. His father was something big in the city . . . possibly one of the Barbican towers.

Basil was tall, strong and his devilish good looks were marred only by the pointed tail and the little red horns on his head. Nigel came from a more modest background. His father had come into some money in the Thirties . . . and some of the notes had got stuck together. He now ran a small sweetshop. When Nigel was eleven his father burnt his mother on an altar — it was necessary to make sacrifices in order to send Nigel to St. Poking.

Basil hated Nigel's guts which he'd seen when Nigel dropped them once in Assembly. Nigel despised everything Basil stood for: the National Anthem, changing a light bulb, pissing against trees, etc. The two of them had been fierce competitors all through school, coming equal top in exams in most subjects. They were both determined, however, to out-do the other over the cricket captaincy. One further reason for this zeal was that it was a school tradition that the captain of cricket escorted the Head's daughter to the end-of-term ball . . . and this particular headmaster had the most gorgeous daughter. She was sixteen. She had long, shiny, straight blonde hair on her head and short, thick, curly black hair on her pet poodle, which she took with her wherever she went. Basil had his sights set on one thing only . . . and that was his double-barrelled shotgun. On the morning of the cricket trial he woke feeling a little smug. 'Fag!' he shouted. A junior entered his chambers. 'Fag, there's a little smug in my bed. I've told you before, we must put smug poison down at nights.'

'Please Mr. Basil, the Head wants to see you urgently!'

'Really? I wonder what that's about?' said Basil with a smile that betrayed the fact that perhaps he already knew. 'Right! You stay here and polish your bottom, Fag. I'll be back shortly.'

Basil found the Head in an abysmal state. It looked like

New Jersey.

'Ah! Ableloins-Skulduggery, do sit down. Cigarette?'

'No. I'll use the chair, Headmaster,' replied Basil.

'Something terrible's happened — Poxdribble's done a bunk!'

'Good lord, Sir, can't somebody wipe it up?'

'He's disappeared. But he's left this note.' Basil smiled inwardly as he read the note which was clearly not in Poxdribble's handwriting:

Dear School,

I've decided to give everything up and become a Trappist monk in Tibet. It is a very strict order with unbreakable vows of silence, so before they begin I would just like to say that Basil Ableloins-Skulduggery should be captain of cricket, go to Oxford and shag the headmaster . . . (silence vows begin now!).

'Notice anything strange, Ableloins-Skulduggery?' asked the Head.

'Yes,' said Basil, 'you haven't got any clothes on!'

'Well, there was that bit in the note . . .'

'I think, with respect Sir, that he was going on to mention your daughter.'

'Really?' The headmaster seemed staggered by this. 'This is most unlike Poxdribble — he was one of our star pupils . . . he was our best cricketer . . . he could have done Oxbridge . . . it's most bizarre. Do you know something, Skulduggery? I smell a rat.'

'It's probably that rat, Sir.'

'Which rat?'

'The one you've got tied to the end of your nose, Sir.'

Poxdribble lay gagged and bound in the school's boiler room. They had come for him in the night. They had put him to sleep, either with drugs or by reading long bits of D. H. Lawrence to him. He didn't see who they were because they had stockings over their heads and top hats over their legs, but he had a shrewd idea that Skulduggery had masterminded the whole thing. Poxdribble struggled and struggled to get free . . . but it was useless. He was tempted to give up, but then he remembered a story from his history lesson about some Scotsman in a cave who had been fired with determination after seeing a spider trying time and time again to build a web. Poxdribble struggled for three or four hours till eventually he had built an enormous web, silky smooth and bejewelled with dewdrops. An idea occurred to him as he sat back to admire his work, little knowing that at that very moment Basil was being made cricket captain for St. Poking-in-the-Undercarriage.

Basil had been first man in to bat and was last man as well. It was the last ball of the match. Basil had made 214 runs. The bowler bowled a fierce bouncer which struck Basil between the eyes and killed him. As if this wasn't bad enough, a jet airliner crashed into the school and blew up in a ball of fire. There were no survivors till Nigel Poxdribble crawled out through a drainage manhole two weeks later. Determined to avenge injustice and to right wrong wherever it happened, Nigel Poxdribble had become the legend that was 'Spiderman'! ! !

Appealing

The secret of appealing is to strike the right balance. Appeal in a half-hearted sort of way and the umpire will feel that it's safe to turn it down without upsetting you. Appeal in a ludicrously over-the-top way and you're likely to upset the umpire, who will turn it down merely out of spite.

If in doubt, it's always worth an appeal — as the old legal saying goes.

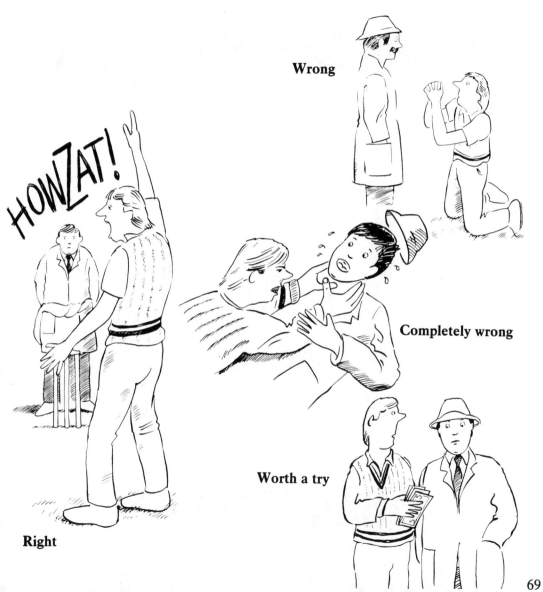

Wrong

Completely wrong

Worth a try

Right

Your Guide to the Cricket

Commentators

Tony Lewis Urbane, soft-spoken Welshman. Once captained England on a three-day tour of the Remote Islands when no one else was available. Highest score 6. Known for his catchphrase, 'Yes, it's absolutely delicious, isn't it, Brian?'

Trevor Bailey Former England and Essex all-rounder, chiefly famous for scoring the longest duck in first-class history. Known for his catchphrase, 'You didn't have to remind me of that again, Brian.'

Brian Johnston Never played cricket in his life, but happened to be hanging around the BBC bar in 1923 when the idea of broadcasting cricket was first thought of by Lord Reith. Brian was mistaken by the producer for Brian 'Taffy' Johnston, the famous Glamorgan leg-breaker chiefly remembered for breaking opposing batsmen's legs.

Christopher Martin-Jenkins Decent-sounding fellow who can be depended on to buy his round in the club bar and always sees both sides of an argument. Yes, nice chap. And Editor of the *Cricketer* magazine which might just do a piece on *Cricket Made Silly*. Bound to – good bloke like CM-J at the helm.

Bill Frindle

Engimatically referred to as the 'Bearded One' by Brian Johnston, Bill Frindle is — statistically speaking — only the second dullest person to broadcast regularly on the BBC, losing by a short head to the announcer who says, 'Entertainment will be provided into the early hours on Radio 2.'

Peter Baxter (producer)

Stanley Baxter's brother. Sits in a BBC outside broadcast unit and has never watched a ball bowled in his life. Known for his catchphrase, 'Well, we seem to have lost transmission there, but fortunately I've still got a TV monitor to watch' — slightly irritating if you're stuck in a traffic jam listening to the radio.

Richie Benaud

Expatriot Australian with. Prominent lower lip, chiefly remarkable for his odd. Speech patterns which involve running one sentence into. Another and then stopping just as he builds up to the vital. Word.

Fred Trueman

Known as 'Fiery Fred' due to his habit of burning down the commentary box as he clumsily lights his pipe. Fred is a blunt-speaking, straight-talking, opinionated Yorkshireman. He was born in the Depression — and he's been pretty pissed off ever since.

Henry Blofeld

Easy-going Old Etonian who happened to stray into the commentary box one day from a P. G. Wodehouse novel and has stayed there ever since.

Cricket on the Radio

Cricket on the radio is immensely popular. Much more popular than actually going to the ground. This is because going to the ground involves travelling miles and miles to pay money to sit yards and yards away from a game that can be called off at a moment's notice should it start to drizzle, which you can hardly see anyway, and which has only odd moments of interest interspersed with hours and hours of boredom.

Whereas cricket on the radio can be enjoyed in the comfort of your own home, for nothing, and involves no more than listening to a few amiable old buffers running on for hours on end, sometimes talking about the match in progress, but for the most part chatting agreeably about other matches, other players, chocolate cakes, pigeons, the weather, the weekend, listeners' letters . . . anything really.

How Do You Become a Cricket Commentator?

Basically there are two routes.

Route 1 involves being born with natural cricket ability. You then have to play well and practise hard at school. Play for the colts, 2nd eleven and first team of the county side of your choice (i.e. the one that chooses you). Get selected for England. Keep your place (more practice and luck involved here), and enjoy a distinguished career making your name a household word. When interviewed on TV and radio, talk in sentences. And then with a bit of luck when your playing days are over the BBC will give you the chance to sit and waffle on about the match in progress, what David Gower ought to do now, this reminds me of Adelaide 1959, etc.

Route 2 involves going to a good school and then working for the BBC sports' department (which is a bit easier).

Qualifications for being a Commentator

The main qualification is to be able to remember euphemisms for 'he's been struck on the testicles', such as, 'that's caught him rather painfully on the upper part of the leg'. Also it is necessary to say things like 'he's in all sorts of trouble', or 'he's at least a yard and half quicker this session', as though you understood them.

Problem Page

It's your bodyline to Geoffrey Borecott, one-time captain of England and two-time captain of Yorkshire.

I've often been told that to be a great batsman the most important thing is your grip. Would you agree?
Oh certainly. You need some sort of grip or travelling bag to carry your bat(s), pads, jumpers and other pieces of equipment. Might I suggest a 'Geoffrey Borecott' cricketer's bag which . . .

No, no. What I mean is, how should you hold the cricket bat when playing?
Well, the best way to get your grip right is to take your bat and lay it on the ground with the handle towards you. Now bend down and take hold of it *by the handle*. Holding it by the other end is next to useless.

No, but *how* should I hold the handle to play the best?
Well, that's my secret. If I told you, you might start challenging for my place.

You're a bit of a selfish bastard, aren't you? Do you ever give anything away?
Why should I tell you that?

You're a bloody disgrace t'Yorkshire.
Oh come on, now you're beginning to sound like Freddie Trueman.

I am Freddie Trueman.

Some Jolly Funny
Cricketing Anecdotes

from Side-splitting
Cricketing Folk

PETER WEST

remembers one epic and bumper wheeze at a Royal dinner

'The venue was the Grosvenor House Hotel . . . the occasion
. . . the MCC's tribute dinner to Sir Robert "no-balls"
Oldfart, who was celebrating 100 glorious years in English
cricket. The guest of honour Princess Anne. Everyone who
was anyone in the cricket world was invited. I wasn't. But I
turned up at the hotel wearing my MCC tie and that worked
wonders. I tied it round a drainpipe at the back, shinned up a
storeroom wall and squeezed in through a first-floor lavatory
window. Who should be in the lavatory but her Royal
Highness. She was in the middle of her you know what, so I
courteously looked the other way. Her Special Branch
body-guard was quick off the mark and had his trousers up in
no time.

Down in the dining room a little later, I set about what I
know best: grovelling and general sycophancy. I'd put on a
special heavy-duty tongue for the occasion. Posing as a poser,
I managed to get onto the number one table. They told me to
get off it and sit on a chair. I found myself between Freddie
Trueman and one of the Royal Ladies-in-Waiting. Freddie
gestured to the waiter . . . ordering two more bottles of wine,
and I set to work on the Lady-in-Waiting, asking her if she
could get hold of a knighthood for me. At that moment the
police burst in and there was a cafuffle on the dance floor. I
think one of the Jewish caterers must have dropped it. Then
the funniest thing happened. Two police officers came up to

me and arrested me for fraud. They said that I was passing myself off as a TV personality and a cricket commentator. How funny . . . they must have the wrong man . . . I'm not a fraud . . . I'm Peter West . . . you know, the cricket commentator and popular TV personality . . . the chap who knows three handy knowledgeable phrases about everything from table tennis to clay pigeon shooting . . . honest, Milud. That's the truth . . . have mercy your honour.'

BRIAN JOHNSTON

selects his funniest moment from many years of test commentaries from Lords

'. . . I think this event is indelibly engraved on my memory . . . We'd laughed so much in the commentary box, I don't think I'll ever forget. It was at Lords . . . or was it the Oval . . . er, no . . . Trent Bridge . . . anyway, it was some cricket ground anyway . . . or was it a swimming pool? Anyway, there we all were in the old BBC box . . . the one they buried Bill Cotton in . . . there was me, Brian Johnston . . . oh, sorry, that is me . . . Anyway, the covers were on and we hadn't seen any cricket all morning. So we took the covers off and, yes, there they were playing cricket out in the middle of the pitch. Then the skies darkened, and before you could say "This job's money for old rope", the heavens opened up and all sorts of gods fell out. It was a typical English summer, rain, rain, rain. We all started cracking zany sorts of jokes. I said, 'If it carries on raining like this . . . everyone's going to get jolly wet!" Everyone roared with laughter. Jim Laker turned to me and said in his usual sardonic way, "Ay, there's enough water out there to prevent a day's cricket!" We all fell about. Richie Benaud quipped, "If we had this much rain in Sydney, the people would look up and say, 'We don't normally have this much rain in Sydney'." Well, by this time we all had tears of laughter rolling down our cheeks . . . We barely had time and energy left after all this laughing to collect our cheques and eat the delicious Victoria sponge sent into us by a Mrs Rose Culshaw of Much Hadham. Then about teatime the rain stopped.

'Jim Laker looked at me, winked in that impish Yorkshire way he has and said, "T'rain's stopped," and I creased up with laughter just in case Jim was making a joke that I didn't understand. Just then it started raining again. "You spoke too soon," I rejoindered pithily. Peals of laughter rang out once again from the commentary box. Just as we were running out of hilarious anecdotes, who should join us in the commentary box but that all-time great British cricketer, Colin Cowdrey. "What about this rain then, Colin?" I asked, and Colin replied, on live radio in front of a listening public which by then must have been in double figures, "Well, Brian, I came out without my mackintosh this morning, and looking back I wish I'd brought it." Quite understandably, we all fell off our chairs laughing at this. But I digress . . . let me get to the meat of my story.

'About six o'clock the skies cleared and the umpire came on to inspect the wicket. He made one of the funniest statements in the history of cricket. He looked up to the sky and said, "Oh sod this, I'm going home." '

RODNEY MARSH

recounts a rumbustious cricketing tale from Down Under

'Melbourne in the middle of summer can be a hellish place. Not only are the temperatures unbearable, but the place is full of Greeks and Lebanese . . . and if that's not bad enough, it's also full of Australians. I recall a particular day in 1980 . . . last day of the test Australia v England . . . the Aussies only needed 55 runs to clinch the game and there were three overs left to play. It was very exciting, and I had a hard-on like a milk-bottle. The empty lager tubes were piling up in the stands . . . and to keep cool the crowd had had to resort to emigrating to Northern Canada. Tension was high, and so was Ian Botham. It was 86 degrees in the sun and 102 degrees in the shade. "Must get that shade fixed," I thought.

'Instead of concentrating on the game and playing up like true professional sportsmen, the Poms were wingeing about some of the Aussie tactics. Lillee had come on with an aluminium bat . . . those poovey Poms kicked up a hell of a fuss when Lillee started bowling with it. The umpire eventually sent him back to the dressing room to get another one. There was a little bit of a tiff when Thomson started using an invisible ball. There's actually nothing in the rules about not using an invisible ball. Officially the ball has to be made out of leather. Well, this ball was made out of dinosaur leather . . . dinosaurs are of course extinct . . . hence the invisibility of the ball. Anyway, the Poms kicked up such a stink about this, that if I'd been Greg Chappell, I'd have kneed each and every one of those Pommy bastards in the goolies. Greg kept his nerve and showed no emotion . . .

Mind you, he was dressed as a giant luminous pink kangaroo, so it was difficult to read any emotions on his face . . . In fact now that I think about it, Greg's outfit came in for some wingeing as well . . . Anyway, it was at this point that the funniest event of the day took place. An old journalist mate of mine, Rob McCluskey, came into the commentary box and told me the story about an Aussie wedding which was called off because someone stole the beer and somebody poked the bride . . . As the disappointed guests were leaving, the hosts rushed out and announced that the wedding was back on saying, "It's OK, everyone. The beer's been returned and the bloke who poked the bride has apologized!" I laughed till my jocks ached.'

Letters to the Ed

•

Dear Ed.,

What is the aim of declaring an innings closed before it is completed? What are the eleven ways a batsman can be got out? Why *is* cricket such a bore?

Yours, A. Cricket Hater

Well, these are all very interesting questions and I often get asked them . . . Let's take the first one. The reason for closing an innings . . .

Dear Ed.,

No, take the last one you smug twat.

Yours, A. Cricket Hater

Oh all right then . . . It's a bore if you're watching it, because everything that happens — which isn't much — happens a long way away from the spectators . . . It's a bore if you're playing, because the game stops every thirty seconds for five minutes while the bowler walks back for his run in. Also, it's usually played when the weather is hot and sunny, which means you're wasting all that lovely summer sunbathing weather when you could be lying on a beach sipping a cocktail or massaging suntan oil into a beautiful girl's shoulders, deftly unclipping her bikini top, turning her over, squirting the oil on to her firm young breasts, making her nipples go erect with excitement. You hear her groan with pleasure, and to your delight and surprise you notice that she has wriggled out of her bikini bottoms and is lying irrestibly naked in the sunshine. I hope that answers your question.

Dear Ed.,

      Hang on. Don't stop there. Carry on . . . I want to hear the rest of it.

   Yours, A. Cricket Hater

Oh, sorry. Well, you declare an innings before it is completed, quite simply to allow the batting side plenty of time to get the fielding side all out and so win.

Dealing with Bouncers

From the point of view of fast bowling, people fall into two groups:

(1) Those who claim that they don't like it.
(2) Those who claim that they do like it.

The latter are usually called 'liars'.

The fact of the matter is, fast bowling is one of life's worst unpleasantnesses, similar to visiting the dentist, watching *The Price is Right*, or washing up ashtrays. It's for this reason that in a club team there is never any shortage of volunteers willing to go in at No. 11. A mistake, this — No. 11 usually comes in just as the fieriest bowler in the team has been brought back, rested and fresh, to 'mop up the tail'.

Dealing with bouncers

Wrong

Right

Completely wrong (but understandable)

Glossary

Some Terms Used in a Cricketing Context

Analysis A calculation designed to show a bowler how badly he has done, making him so depressed he goes to see a psychiatrist.

Bails The things belonging to a batsman which the bowler aims to knock off. (Not to be confused with *Balls*, which are the deliveries the bowler uses in his attempt.)

Bail System of releasing a criminal between arrest and trial so that he has the chance to do a few more crimes before being sent to prison.

Batsman A powerful hitter of the ball, dressed in white trousers.

Batman More powerful person dressed in blue tights and very friendly with a boy called Robin.

Vatman Even more powerful man dressed in a grey suit and friendly with no one.

Body-Line Controversial way of bowling developed by England in order to stop Donald Bradman. The idea was not really to hit his body, as the Australians alleged. More properly called 'Leg Theory'. The theory being that Bradman wouldn't do so well if his legs were broken.

Bouncer (1) Psychopath in possession of evening dress. (2) Short-pitched delivery bowled by psychopath who has taken off evening dress and put on white flannels.

Box Just what it says it is. A small box for putting your genitalia in when you go in to bat. Make sure you lock the box and put it somewhere safe. Genitals are hard to come by . . . especially if you haven't got any.

Captain Birds Eye   Elderly actor who should be playing King Lear, reduced to impersonating an old sailor so more people eat frozen peas. Sad, isn't it?

Captain's Cabin   A pub in London just off Lower Regent Street.

Captain's Innings   Match-saving innings in which captain bats for a day and a half to force a draw.

Carrying your bat   (1) Technical term for opening the innings and being not out at the end. (2) The best way of getting your bat to the centre of the field where you will need it when batting. Special bat-shaped shoulder bags are also available if you can't be bothered.

Cricket season   Time of the year when you notice how wet the English climate is.

Cricket bats   None. Presumably too short-sighted (see England selectors).

Straight bat   Bat with heterosexual tendencies.

Daisy cutter   A bowler who works part-time in a beef-processing plant or slaughterhouse.

Duck   Innings of 0.

Fair play   Cricket has strict rules of play. Most people are familiar with the tremendously British phrases 'Come on – play the game' and 'Hey, that's not cricket'.
These are employed when a British team is being outclassed in all departments by some skilled foreigners.

Golden duck   Innings of 0 lasting just one ball.

Lame duck   Industry or service almost completely lacking customers, out-of-date, losing money and only kept in business by massive subsidy (e.g. County Championship).

Gentlemen & Players   An old distinction in English cricket which is no longer observed as there are so few gentlemen left in the game and hardly any who can play very well either.

Googly An off-break which looks like a leg-break, or possibly the other way round. Said to be invented by Reginald Bosanquet's father (said on *News at Ten*).

Googlies The plural of above, much appreciated by the Benny Hill School of Comedy, as in the expressions: 'He hit his googlies with a straight bat'; 'I've never seen such magnificent googlies'; 'The *Benny Hill Show* is a load of balls'.

Howzat Third person singular of the Latin verb *howzo*, *howzas* etc., which means to jump up and down waving your arms about while trying to pretend to the umpire that you think someone has just got out.

In-swinger Man with keys to Porsche at a wife-swapping party.

Out-swinger Man who wears white Y-fronts and Vyella shirts.

Leg-bye Famous quotation from Sir Douglas Bader.

Lords Nickname of a pub in St John's Wood, London, whose full name is the Lord's Tavern. They do very good pub grub, including the best ploughman's lunch in South-East England. The disadvantages are the large number of ploughs parked outside at lunchtime and a bunch of noisy yobbos playing cricket in the enormous beer garden at the back.

Military Medium A not quite fast pace of bowling named after Brigadier Doris Stokes.

Maiden Young girl or virgin.

Virgin Girl who is inexperienced sexually, mentioned in song by Madonna.

Virgin over Madonna.

Maiden over 6 balls during which nothing happens (c.f. Madonna).

Nightwatchman (1) Some poor schmuck from low down the order, brought in when things are getting hairy towards the end of a day's play. (2) An old man who sleeps in a hut while his employers' premises are burgled.

No balls   Descriptive of the Italian Army, Arsenal defence etc.

National Sport   Rather pointless description of cricket, football etc. with reference to England whose population also plays rugby, athletics, snooker, bowls, swimming, tennis, riding, basketball, and so on.

Schoolboy cricket   Played by schoolboys.

Club cricket   Played by overgrown schoolboys.

First-class cricket   Played by professional cricketers to make money out of schoolboys and overgrown schoolboys.

Short middle leg   Self-effacing term for the male member. Opposite of such terms as 'long fat pink knobbly middle leg', 'boner before wicket' etc.

Sightscreen   Large moveable wooden fence behind which lovers can have it off without distracting the batsman.

Stumped   You are 'stumped' if someone asks you a question such as 'What is the capital of Malawi?' or 'How does Terry Wogan get away with it?'

Sweep   Sooty's doggy friend who never speaks but occasionally utters a high-pitched squeal . . . one of the consequences of having Harry Corbett's hand up your bum.

Test match   A game played between two countries. So-called because five days of the slowest game known to man is enough to test anyone's patience.

Third man   (1) Someone who follows cricket on Radio 3. (2) Film in which the girl walks past the man at the end. (3) Fielding position in which the ball goes past the man because he was only put there in the first place because he was such a bad fielder.

Tip-and-run   (1) Informal form of cricket played mainly by schoolboys. (2) Official government policy for dealing with nuclear waste.

Run Out Of ideas for this page.

Some Terms Never Used in a Cricketing Context

Hilary Famous Englishman. The first man ever to conquer the greatest challenge on earth – being born with a girl's name.

Cor Anglais Expression used by gay Frenchman on seeing pretty English boy.

Iceberg Founder member of the Jewish plot to sink the *Titanic*.

Iceberg Lettuce Founder member of the Jewish vegetarian plot to sink the *Titanic*.

Great Wall of China The only man-made object visible from the moon.

The Moon The only satellite of Earth visible from the Great Wall of China.

Joan Collins The only man-made object visible in *Dynasty*.

Suspended Animation The Arsenal mid-field.

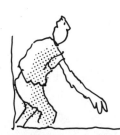

Answers

Across 1/Marylebone 6/Swing 8/Near miss 11/Kit 12/Over
13/Rebel 14/Leg 15/Retreat 16/Off 18/Interstate 20/Lulls
22/Talent 25/Easy single 27/Even 28/Elevenses 29/Ashes

Down 1/Minor counties 2/Yorker 3/Exit 4/Essential 5/Six
7/Googlies 9/Milestone 10/Sobers 14/Level 17/Fielders 19/Turn
21/Lillee 23/Tames 24/Ryder 26/Idea